you took me in

me in

poems of life, loss, and love

anthology of selected verse

george f. harris jr.

you took me in

© 2024 by Windfalls Productions LLC

Published in Columbia, Tennessee, by Windfalls Productions LLC. Information regarding this book and other titles from Windfalls Productions may be found at www.windfallsproductions.com.

ISBN: 979-8-218-25063-8

I dedicate this collection of thoughts to my Father in heaven, from whom inspiration for these words has flowed. I also dedicate it to my earthly father and my wife, who supported me in this endeavor.

Table of Contents

Introduction

Although I was born in Poughkeepsie, New York, I hail from New Jersey, where I was a high school and junior high teacher for thirty-two years. Interestingly, I taught trade skills and broadcasting, subjects that had nothing to do with English, composition, grammar, or creative writing, yet here I am. Wisdom and faith have taught me that where God leads, I will follow. These poems came from my pen, but I did not command the words that filled my thoughts. Only our Lord and Savior, Jesus Christ, could give someone who was only fair in English the inspiration and eloquence found herein.

It seems to me, being on this earth for seventy-three years, that the human race has slowly deteriorated to a lower morale. Some of these poems came to mind at the most difficult times for many people. Some came to me at what seemed my lowest of times. But as the words came out of my head and onto the paper, I felt that God was putting these words onto the paper Himself. I would get a feeling of relief and calmness as the poem would come to the end and I could go on with life. Obviously, not all the poems deal with pain or hurt. Many of them deal with joy, compassion, and love. Those poems are my favorite because I feel God talking to me to show His love for me.

No matter what this world throws at me, God is always with me. Through His Son who sacrificed Himself for us, He brought us into His family for eternity. No matter what this world throws at us, the hope of life is and always will be with the love of our Father and His Son.

I hope that at least one of these poems will affect you and show you the same hope and love that has affected me. I have heard that no matter how big the storm, if the Lord is in it, that is the best place to be. No matter how far out on a thin limb the Lord calls us, the safest place to be is sitting on the limb with the Lord. So here I sit. I pray you will join us.

Be blessed!
George F. Harris Jr.

"I can do everything through Christ, who gives me strength."
Philippians 4:13

9

Family

The feeling of warmth, joy, and a sense of belonging was rare in my earliest childhood years. When I was around two years old, my brother and I were abandoned, as well as my two sisters, whom I didn't even know existed until I was an adult. My brother and I were adopted by two loving, Christian parents when I was five.

The first poem in this section, "You Took Me In," was not only the first one I wrote, but it is written in honor of my loving, Christian, adoptive parents, who gave generously and sacrificed for us. Reaching out and inviting a child to become family comes with great reward as well as great risks. When you adopt abandoned children, they bring with them emotional baggage, like grudges, fear, and anger. When I think back through the years, I realize the chances parents like mine take when they reach out and adopt a child. They take the chance of not knowing how it will turn out, or what the child's circumstances were that would lead them to think life is always this way. I don't even remember if I knew the meaning of Christmas until I was five years old.

Obviously, this section reflects on how I felt as my life situations unfolded. Some brought joy, some great pain, and others crumbled before my blinded eyes. I truly hope that these will help you in your relationship with your family before it is too late.

"God places the lonely in families."
Psalms 68:6a

You Took Me In

You took me in when I was a kid,
under the dash I slid and hid.
I didn't know what was going on,
at that time, I was no one's son.
We went from one house to the next,
it seemed to me like we were hexed.
But you took a chance and took us in,
and that's how I learned about love within.
At that time, you gave me my life back,
now in this world there's nothing I lack.
Thank you for the life I'm living,
full of laughter, full of giving.
Thank you for showing us the way,
and I hope that I will never stray.

Dad

You've been my best friend all my life,
you've always been there through any strife.
I could always count on your wisdom and love,
many times, it'd feel like it came from above.
This is just a small token of my love for you,
I don't know what I would have done without you.

Thank You

I came into this world unloved, uncared,
then suddenly you both were there.
To give us direction, to give us love,
I feel you both were sent from above.
To give us a chance in this hard life,
to teach us how to survive this strife.
With your loving and caring tones,
for once in our lives, we weren't alone.
You taught us how to love each other,
how to care and help one another.
When I'm in pain, you're always there,
when I need advice, you're always fair.
Thank you for your love, thank you for your life,
thank you for helping me see the light.
Your wisdom always pointed me the way,
it kept me from slipping or going astray.
I could always count on you when I needed you most,
you were always there from coast to coast.
God knew what he was doing when He gave us to you,
He knew what we needed, and that was you two.
I love you guys more than I can say,
I love you more as each day slips away.
Thank you for taking us when you did,
thank you for being Mom and Dad to this kid.

We Were Brothers

We were brothers, yet so far apart,
we had a bad beginning right from the start.
We were fortunate to be adopted by such loving parents,
we received much love from them, that's apparent.
But what happened to us as we grew up?
I went one way and you went the other.
For many—too many—years we lost touch,
I wasn't happy about that, not very much.
But I still loved you, that I can tell,
I hoped one day you'd come back, and all would be well.
I prayed you'd wake up and look at your life,
I would be there to help you see the light.
Why wouldn't you listen to what we had to say?
why did you insist to have your own way?
I'm sorry I couldn't help you see and understand,
that you could, against your bad habits, make a stand.
Each night I prayed you'd come back into our arms,
knowing that you were still loved, and we'd snatch you from harm.
We never got that chance, I'm sorry to say,
but God knew better and did it His way.
So I hope you can forgive me for failing you that way,
and know that, where you are, you'll never stray.
I love you, Jim, don't ever forget,
you're at a better place, with no pain and no fret.

Miss My Family

I miss my family so very much,
it's hard not to be able to keep in touch.
You gave me love when I had none,
you made me feel like I was number one.
You didn't have to take us in,
but you did and showed us love within.
You showed us how to take care of others,
how to trust everyone like sisters and brothers.
You taught us not to be self-centered,
and give to others services rendered.
I'd like to think I've acquired a little of you,
and carry it through my life, too.
So thank you for taking such a chance,
for with my life you enhanced.
But God has you now, and that is true,
and one day I, too, will be up there with you.

In Loving Memory

We all benefited with your presence here,
with you gone, we shed many a tear.
God has another plan for you two,
peace be with you until we follow you.

My Child's Eyes

In my child's eyes I do no wrong,
through the darkest night and earliest dawn.
My child runs to me as I walk through the door,
and hugs me tightly on the way to the floor.
We wrestle and roll around for a while,
I'm so proud to be the parent of this child.
We promise together we'll never part,
but deep down I know, one day it'll start.
The day my child wants freedom and goes astray,
no matter how hard I beg and offer promises to stay.
I hope the past will always remind,
my child will always and forever be mine.
I love you so very much,
please remember to keep in touch.

Motherhood

God has blessed me to be a mother,
I join the blessed of many others.
My soul glorifies the Lord and rejoices in God, my Savior,
He has been mindful of his servant's humble behavior.
His mercy extends to those who love Him,
from generation to generation is where it's been.
I love the chance to show His love,
by His child sent from above.
So, Father I hope I can handle the mission,
of joining the rest, of following Your commission.

Dedicated to all mothers.

Mother

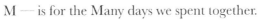

M — is for the Many days we spent together.
O — is for all she Offered in all kinds of weather.
T — is for the Tough times you brought me through.
H — is for all the Helpful advice given to me by you.
E — is for Everyday you said you loved me.
R — is for the Right way you taught me to help my soul.

Put them all together, and they spell MOTHER.
The one person who means the world to me.

Father

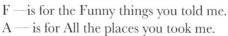

F —is for the Funny things you told me.
A — is for All the places you took me.
T —is for the many Things you taught me.
H —is for the Help you used to give me.
E —is for Everyday you said you loved me.
R —is for the Right way you taught me to live.

Put them all together and they spell FATHER.
The one person who means the world to me.

Remembering You

When I'm sitting by myself I start thinking about you,
then I know why I feel so blue.
I loved you so much, but hardly told you so,
when my head starts spinning, I don't know where to go.
All I do is remember what it was like
to walk alongside you on our many hikes.
You worked so hard to take care of us,
to know, with you, I can always trust.
Even though you're gone, and I can't touch you,
everything you taught me I know is true.
I hope my life can reflect your love,
I know you're looking down from above.
Thank you so much for bringing me into your life,
thank you so much for relieving my strife.

I Miss Your Smile

I miss your smile and your stern jaw,
I miss how you used to lay down the law.
I miss the stories you used to tell,
and how you would say, "All is well."
I miss the calls each week on the phone,
they would always cheer me up, especially when alone.
Your jokes would put a smile on my face,
and my troubles would disappear without a trace.
I wish I had spent more time with you,
especially telling you how much I love you.
But now that'll wait until we meet again,
and when that'll be, only God knows when.
Just know that I truly love you,
and one day, together, you can tell me, too.

Dad: My Friend/ My Buddy

You've been my buddy all my life,
you've always been through many a strife.
I could always depend on your listening ears,
and after that I had no fears.
You could always put a smile on my face,
before a mistake was made in haste.
Even when I stumbled and did wrong,
in my heart you'd leave a song.
You leave behind all that strife,
you are missed in this life.
You left a legacy that can't be filled,
there's no one here who can match your skill.
Where you are there is no pain,
there is no storm, or even rain.
Enjoy what you looked for all your life,
enjoy the love, enjoy the light.
I say goodbye until we meet again,
when I also will have no strife nor pain.

Lorna

Even though you're just a dog, I love you so much,
it's hard to believe I'll never again feel your touch.
Why did you have to leave me? Why couldn't you wait?
I'm sorry I was away. I'm sorry I was so late.
I tried to, but I couldn't get home fast enough.
I'm truly sorry, I love you so much!

Dad

George F. Harris, Sr.
Yeoman First Class, U.S. Coast Guard, and Dad

They met in Sunday School class in their hometown of Westville, New Jersey, and they married on May 22, 1943. On their wedding day, six-foot-five inch George Sr., decked out in his US Coast Guard uniform, towered over his beautiful bride, five-foot-two inch Rose. Within twenty-four hours of their wedding, George was deployed to San Diego, California, where he would serve aboard the USS Hutchinson for the remainder of WWII.

As the lead Yeoman for the USS Hutchinson, Dad produced the daily schedule, the ship's newsletter, and other required publications into which he sometimes injected his subtle, dry humor for all to enjoy. Included in this section are a few poems he wrote during his time onboard the ship. Traveling throughout the South Pacific, he would write to my mother about his experiences in ports such as Singapore, Tahiti, and Australia. After crossing the equator and undergoing the traditional seaman's ritual, he was awarded the honor of "Shellback" (one who has crossed the equator) from the Ancient Order of the Deep. While not being in the thickest of the war action, the USS Hutchinson endured a fair amount of shelling during its tenure.

After the war ended, Dad entered a banking career, eventually becoming the President of the National Bank of Mantua. After his retirement, that bank became Wells Fargo Bank. Rose worked as a bookkeeper until they adopted my brother and me. She then settled into a full-time career as a stay-at-home Mom. Our family was very active at the Lutheran Church across the street from our family home. Once we were grown and Dad retired, he took Mom on a charted course on a container ship cruise to visit several of the places about which he had written in his letters all those many years ago.

In their later years, they moved to a Christian retirement community in Florida. When I would visit them, Dad always enjoyed beating me in a round of golf. Despite that, I still considered him my best friend!

Bad Haircut

'Tis seldom that I in poetry speak,
and rarely do I complain.
But now in verse 'tis pity I seek,
'cause my ear is filled with pain.

'Twas a bright, warm Sunday, not long past,
(while cruising in tropic clime)
I found that my hair had grown too fast
and 'twas nigh hair-cutting time.

So I hied me aft to the fantail
where in the sunshine so bright
Kates showed me a chair by the liferail,
and therefor began my plight.

He snipped some hair from on top my head,
and then with a vicious leer
he snipped some hair on the side of my head
near my unsuspecting ear.

Nearer and Nearer to my ear he came,
then with a howl of delight
he snipped the very top of the same—
the ear about which I write.

An awful leap from that chair I gave
and in loud anguish cried.
I began to curse and rant and rave
o, I was fit to be tied!

I told him what I thought of the men
who the barber profession plied,
and swore that I would never again
have my hair cut on the side.

Bugs

(With all due apologies to Rudyard Kipling)

We watch them crawl- crawl- crawlin' o'er the bread and pie,
then crawl- crawl- crawl-crawlin' back again
(bugs- bugs- bugs- bugs crawlin' on the food we eat)
and there's no flit upon the ship.

Seven-six-eleven-five bugs on every bit o' bread,
four-eleven-seventeen crawlin' on the pie crust too
(bugs- bugs- bugs- bugs crawlin' on the food we eat)
and there's no flit upon the ship.

Don't- don't- don't- don't- think about tomorrow's chow
(bugs- bugs- bugs- bugs crawlin' on the food we eat)
men- men- men- men- men go mad with watchin' 'em,
and there's no flit on board the ship.

Count-count-count-count all the bread and pie you ate
and then think of all the food you're gonna eat
(bugs- bugs- bugs- bugs crawlin' on the food we eat)
and there's no flit on board the ship.

We-can-stick-out-water that is full of salt
but-not- not- not- not the crawlin sight of 'em
(bugs- bugs- bugs- bugs crawlin' on the food we eat)
and there's no flit on board the ship.

It's-not-bad when we don't get pie or bread,
but-those-two-items brings them by the millions

(bugs- bugs- bugs- bugs crawlin' on the food we eat)
and there's no flit on board the ship.

I-have-sailed-ten months in hell and certify
It's-not-brimstone-dark or anything,
(bugs- bugs- bugs- bugs crawlin' on the food we eat)
and there's no flit on board the ship.

Where's The Snow

Who would have thought, two years ago,
that on this Christmas day
I would be sailing the calm blue sea
ten thousand miles away.

'Twas Christmas, nineteen forty two
(the snow lay deep and white)
that I dreamed of an isle, tropical, too,
with a mellow moon at night.

I saw a lazy surf at play
against a brilliant strand,
while dusky maids spent the day
dancing to music, on the sand.

I made up my mind that I wouldn't stay
where winter ruled the land,
but would hie me away, by next Christmas Day
and spend a Christmas on that strand.

Well, I'm down here now, in a tropical clime
and Christmas is here again
and tho' I tell you this in rhyme
I mean every word my friend.

The breeze isn't balmy, it's terrifically hot,
This tropical clime is no go.
So please let me, by next Christmas Day
be back in the land of the snow.

Wife/Partner

There is no better opportunity for finding consistent peace and joy than finding the perfect life partner. Until, of course, you realize that neither that life partner, nor you, is actually "perfect." Listening to God's direction in choosing the right spouse means everything! The wrong relationship can bring more heartache and pain for all concerned than the holy vows of marriage can sustain. Loving friends and family see your missteps, but are afraid to interfere. On goes the misery. On goes your unwillingness to accept that all you had hoped for is over.

One day, when the sky opened and God's choice for me appeared, she was not as perfect as I had envisioned. To my surprise, through the years, she has proven to be the very best teammate I could have ever imagined. Patience, my friend: Patience.

"The man who finds a wife finds a treasure,
and he receives favor from the LORD."
Proverbs 18:22

"As the Scriptures say, "A man leaves his father and mother
and is joined to his wife, and the two are united into one."
Ephesians 5:/Genesis 2:24

Two-Year Anniversary

It's hard to believe it's been two years,
when we came together and wiped our tears.
My whole world changed when you came into my life,
I began to laugh when you became my wife.
You're the best thing that has ever happened to me,
God knew from the start,
even though we could not see.
You're my best friend, the love of my life,
together we'll live through any strife.
I love you sweetheart, don't ever forget,
these years are just the beginning,
the best is to come yet.

My Wife

Three years ago, through all my strife,
did I ever think that you'd be my wife?
But God had this plan all along,
that we'd be together making our songs.
He knew our loneliness and despair,
and like Adam and Eve, made us a pair.
I thank you, God, for my wife,
I thank you, God, she's in my life.

I Love You More

Seven years ago we were bonded together,
to live this life through all kinds of weather.
I pray that we will continue forever,
my love for you will never waver.
I love you more than words can say,
I love you more in every way.

A Wife

A wife of noble character who can find?
she is worth far more than rubies or wine.
She will do anything without being asked,
she works hard at everything, whatever the task.
She's faithful and true and is always there,
and if anyone is against you, they better beware!
She's very protective, like a bear and her cub,
and the meals she cooks are more than just grub!
When you find this person, she makes a perfect mate,
but when it comes to dinner, don't be late!

Blessed

God blessed me when He gave me you as my wife,
loneliness disappeared when you came into my life.
I was going down this broken road,
not knowing what to do,
but the road brightened when He gave me you.
I know that whatever life throws at me,
you are by my side,
and together we'll get through it and not need to hide.
Father, thank you for your gift to me, my wife,
thank you for showing me the light.
So, my love, I have your back wherever we go,
and never forget and always know.
I love you so much, it will never fail,
it will always be fresh and never be stale.

You Light Up My Life

You light up my world, you light up my life,
I'm so happy you became my wife.
I can never imagine living without you,
I'm sure I would always be blue.
You always make sure I have all my needs,
in a field of wheat, you're like a gentle breeze.
God had a plan when He sent you my way,
He called down an angel, and with you I'll stay.
So always know my feelings for you,
my love will always, always be true.
You're my inspiration, you're my strength,
to my Father, I give Him thanks.
My love for you runs so deep,
I finally realized it is you I seek.
I hear your voice every day,
I hear your voice in every way.
I see you in my mind in everything I do,
I see your image day and night, too.
When I go to sleep, I think of you,
when I wake up, I'm glad you're there, too.
My only wish is to grow old with you,
I love you so much, I truly do.
Please, dear God, help us to be,
together forever, the only way to be.

To The One I Love

To the one I love,
you were sent from above.
The way you stole my heart,
I hope we'll never part.
Thanks for loving me the way you do,
Happy Valentine's Day to the love that's true!

To My Valentine

What can I do, what can I say?
help me, Father, show me the way.
Show me my love, show me my mate,
tell me, Father, what is my fate.
I prayed to God to end my fear,
then suddenly you appeared!
I thank God He gave you to me,
now my life from loneliness is free.
Now at this most special time,
won't you be my Valentine?

More Than Words Can Say

I love you more than words can say,
I love you more in every way.
I love you more each and every day,
I love you more, why won't you stay?
I tell you so over and over again,
as many times as the summer has rain.

Friends

If you have not experienced the wonderful relationship called friendship, you may not grasp the need for a separate section honoring the loss of friends. A very close friend is the deepest, most cherished of all personal connections, even closer and stronger than family. A true friend is someone who walks life with you without judgement, laughs and cries with you, and simply listens as you pour out your heart. The loss of a close friend can stimulate a mixture of emotions, from momentary sadness to deep depression, especially when the loss is someone who has been a trusted best friend your entire life. Thoughts of living life without that friend are almost unbearable. Favorite moments and even disagreements become fondest memories that you lean on to find strength to move on, knowing God has a different plan for your life than for theirs. Perhaps these poems will help you to recall memories of close friends, whether they are alive or waiting for you at Heaven's gates.

"Greater love has no one than this:
to lay down one's life for one's friends."
John 15:13

"Love prospers when a fault is forgiven,
but dwelling on it separates close friends."
Proverbs 17:9

Bruce

Bruce is at peace in God's arms,
he is free from pain and free from harm.
The big O' we'll never forget,
he had a heart of gold, I'm so glad we met.
He'll be greatly missed as the days go by,
but if you want to see him, just look into the sky.
He'll always be there, either night or day,
with that big smile that'll never fade.
Sorry, big guy, that God called you home,
but don't you fret, you won't be alone.
We love you, man, and we always will,
you made our hearts warm and our anxiety still.
Goodbye, dear friend, till we meet again,
only God knows how, and He knows when.

A Tribute To A Friend

True friends are hard to find,
true friends are always kind.
They don't judge you, they don't scorn,
true friendship is never torn.
When you feel low, down, and out,
friends are there to help you out.
Bob was just that kind of friend,
his love and caring had no end.
He'd always lend to you an ear,
he seemed to know and have no fear.
He never judged or put you down,
his smile would always bring you around.
We're going to miss you, my dear friend,
but your smile, your laughter will never end.

Friends

Friends are important when you're in need,
for whatever reason, for whatever deed.
Whether from across the street or from afar,
a friend is important, they're your shining star.
They stay with you through thick and thin,
and the only outcome will be a win.
So whatever you do, or wherever you are,
hold tight to that friend, hold tight to your star.

I Never Said
I Love You

I never said I loved you, but I do,
I hope that in some way you knew.
I always saw you as my second father,
I hope that to you it wasn't a bother.
We've known each other since I was a kid,
our feelings for each other were never hid.
We've celebrated many a holiday together,
in many a day, in all kinds of weather.
Even when we were apart by many miles,
when we did get together, there were many smiles.
Now you have gone to a special place,
where there is no pain, only smiles on the face.
so be assured that we'll meet again,
Only God will know where, and He knows when.
I love you, Pop, and I still do,
You're in God's arms, I'll see you soon.

Dedicated to Robert Thompson SR,
who was like a second Dad to me.

47

Friends Forever

We were together at the dance,
at all the games we took a chance.
We suffered together in all kinds of weather,
no matter what we did, we stuck together.
Five days a week we saw each other,
all through the winter together we'd shutter.
We always had each other's back,
whether we knew it or not, that was the fact.
So just remember this and remember it well,
for the rest of our lives we will always tell.
Our friendship for each other will never end,
you will always be my best friend.

*"Finally, dear brothers and sisters, we ask you to pray for us.
Pray that the Lord's message will spread rapidly and be honored
wherever it goes, just as when it came to you."*
2 Thessalonians 3:1

Mission Trips

Way back in the 1970s, a speaker at church enlightened me about the true joy of mission trips. When asked if I was interested in participating, I jumped at the opportunity. I have gone every year for almost fifty years since I accepted that invitation. I feel strongly about missions here in the United States, so I work with various churches based in New Jersey, Pennsylvania, and Delaware, where we help build or repair residential structures. Although unexpected conditions and personalities make these faith-based adventures unpredictable and challenging at times, I highly recommend the rewarding experience and opportunity of bringing pure delight to the recipients of our labor of love. It's my belief that if more people would donate their time to help others instead of bullying and harming them, they would discover the joy that helping people brings. This calling is not from man but from our Father in heaven. We are expected to help each other in this life, and the sooner we start, the better this world will be.

During my first year of college, I became the technical manager for a Christian singing group known as the King's Crusaders. We met at a small church in New Jersey. This cheerful and lively group, led by Pastor Carlton Bodine, traveled locally and nationally leading worship at evening services. Group participants, who were typically high school age, spent weekends and school break weeks packing into trucks and cars ready for an adventure. Though schedules were stressful at times, many of us came to know the Lord as we journeyed to planned destinations and through life's challenges. Because poem words never give advance notice, I kept a pencil and paper handy so that the poems could be captured in the moment. The poem titled "Showing Us the Way" is a good example of Pastor's continual counseling and shepherding us through life's many trials.

"So the message about the Lord spread widely
and had a powerful effect."
Acts 19:20

"And I have been a constant example of how you can help those in need by working hard. You should remember the words of the Lord Jesus: 'It is more blessed to give than to receive.'"
Acts 20:35

"He said to his disciples, 'The harvest is great, but the workers are few. So pray to the Lord who is in charge of the harvest; ask Him to send more workers into his fields.'"
Matthew 9:37-38

Thank You, Father

Thank you, Father, for this trip,
for words you put upon my lips.
To help other people who are in need,
to look at life and take heed.
Life is short, too short to waste,
the love of God we must taste.
To do this, our neighbor we must love,
all things we need are sent from above.
So help us Lord to do what's right,
and help all those who come in our sight.
Give us the wisdom, give us the skills,
to give these people a little thrill.
Thank you, Father, for this chance,
for others and our lives to enhance.

Mission

We're here, dear Lord, to do your will,
in any way or by any skill.
To praise Your name and glorify You,
to share Your love and Your mercy, too.
We wish for the world to know Your name,
by the work we do and our love the same.
We leave our loved ones and travel miles
to help the needy and have them smile.
Be with us, Father, and keep us safe
till we arrive at home to our comfort place.

Lord, We're Here To Praise

Lord, we're here to praise your name,
all together, all the same.
We thank you, Lord, for getting us here,
we had no concerns; we had no fears.
We knew that all along you were with us,
there was no mess, there was no fuss.
We want to be righteous just like you are,
for we know that will take us far.
Thank you much for all your love,
our love back to you up above.

Showing Us The Way

Thank you, Lord, for showing us the way,
thank you, Lord, for helping us to stay
On the course you have willed and drawn up,
through the good and the bad, you made us tough.
You helped us to see the direction to go,
and you kept us focused, how, I don't know.
In this world, it's tough to stay straight,
with You, at times, we must wait.
Life is quick, we want it now,
we need to slow down somehow.
Thank you, Lord, for showing us the way,
thank you, Lord for helping us to stay.

To Win The Fight

God, we're here tonight to try and win the fight,
thank you, Lord, for showing us the light.
You were with us in the cars,
even though there were no stars.
We are glad to be here,
with you we have no fear.
Even though it's raining now,
you can still show us how.
Come into someone's heart,
and let them get their first start.
Alone it's hard to fight sin,
but it's easier if you know Him.
Now come back on the rebound,
and jump up off the ground.
Now that you've come to know Him,
we can try to destroy sin.
No matter where you are,
no matter how far.
For us He paid the price,
our dear Lord Jesus Christ.
We believe in Him, we do,
so why not you?

Comfort

We are on this earth for only a short period of time. With the loss of someone we love, whether it is family or friend, we move through the cycle of death, each in our own way. Acceptance comes more gently for some, while others become stuck in the denial or anger phase for many years. Many times, we don't understand why, especially if that person is young. In Christ, our sorrow should only be for our own loss. We can find peace knowing our loved one is held securely in the everlasting arms of Jesus. And knowing this, as a Christian, we believe that when we go, we will see them again in the afterlife.

These poems of comfort filled my thoughts after certain people in my life slipped from earth's grasp and went home to the Lord. I felt that God was calling them home to be with Him. Upon knowing the fulfillment of this truth, I look forward to seeing them again when I go home to be with the Lord.

"Death is swallowed up in victory. O death, where is your victory?
O death, where is your sting?"
1 Corinthians 15: 54b, 55

"We are confident that as you share in our sufferings,
you will also share in the comfort God gives us."
2 Corinthians 1:7

Come Home, Faithful Servant

Come home, faithful servant, come home,
you don't have to fear being alone.
Good and faithful servant, come home to me,
look at the room I've prepared for thee.
You've run the race, and you've run it well,
you've fought against the angels from hell.
You have fought your fight, I'm proud of your life,
now come home to Me, just follow the light.
Many times you did well going up against Satan,
and for you, more than once, there was no haven.
So good and faithful servant, come home to me,
look at the room I've prepared for thee.

Come Into My Arms

Come, my child, come into my arms,
come, my child, I mean you no harm.
You lived the life, and you lived it well,
you did my will, and I can tell.
You fought the fight, and I must say,
you fought so well; you chased sin away.
You did well, and I'm proud of you,
I have this room made just for you.
So come into my arms, let me hold you tight,
you've won the battle; you've won the fight.
No more pain and no more tears,
no more wants and no more fears.
Come, my child, come into my arms,
come my child, don't be alarmed.
Come, my child, where there is no harm,
there is no dusk, and there is no dawn.

Take Me Home

Take me home, dear Father, take me home,
I'm sick and tired of being alone.
All I do anymore is argue and fight,
I can't seem to be able to see the light.
Only you, Father, can straighten things out,
whatever happens, it's your will; I have no doubt.

Welcome Home

Welcome, my faithful one, welcome home,
don't you fret, you're not alone.
You've fought the good fight through these years,
you've laughed and shed many tears.
But you persevered, not gone astray,
you've hung in there all the way.
You ran it well, you finished the race,
come on home, come with haste.
Even though at times you fell,
you did your job and did it well.
Through all obstacles, you kept the faith,
no time to delay, no time to wait.
You never altered, you withstood the test,
so welcome home, it's time to rest.

My Son

My son, my son, what can I say,
he helped me pass the time away.
We would talk a long time about his life,
we would try to solve life's many a strife.
We would have fun to play, just a simple game,
we would talk about our dreams to see if they were the same.
He was my baby, I loved him so much,
many times, I wish I could feel his touch.
Now God has taken my baby away,
it is so hard to let go, needless to say.
But I know in my heart he is in good hands,
and I know one day we will be together again.

Dedicated to Rob Spencer who went home to Jesus in 2014.

Heroes
Civilian/Military

There was a time in my life that I wanted to become part of an elite group called emergency responders. With my father participating as a volunteer firefighter, I always thought I would have an "in". However, politics beyond my control squashed my chances of joining the group. My respect for firefighters in general never faltered. Each time I heard news of a disaster, whether it be military conflicts abroad or a house fire closer to home, I would again have words flood my mind and poems emerge. Not knowing them personally, I want to dedicate this section to honor the bravery and humility often displayed by those who run to the fire and save lives for us all, and emergency responders everywhere. If more would show the same character and selflessness, as Christ did for us and directs us to do, the world would be a better place to live.

"A spiritual gift is given to each of us so we can help each other."
1 Corinthians 12:7

"When God's people are in need, be ready to help them.
Always be eager to practice hospitality."
Romans 12:13

Fallen Emergency Responders

You risk your life for people you don't even know,
when the alarm goes off, you're on the go.
You never know what'll happen or what you'll face,
but you pray for strength and for God's grace.
Many times, you'll make it and come home to us all,
but sometimes you don't, and some of you will fall.
Your commitment was real and never strayed,
and your strength was from God, all the way.
Goodbye, dear friend, you'll be missed a great deal,
and the love you gave we continue to feel.
Dear God, we pray, in Your arms they're within,
we wait for the day when we're together again.
Thank you for your commitment that will never part,
this thank you is for you, from the bottom of my heart.

You Fight For Us

They fought for our freedom and gave us their life,
they traveled many miles leaving their family and their wife.
They fought long and hard to free us all,
you were always around and always on call.
You'll always be remembered and your spirit lives on,
thank you for your sacrifice, sorry you're gone.
Thank you for your commitment that will never part,
thank you for a chance for a brand-new start.

The Greatest Sacrifice

You fight for our freedom; you give us your life,
you leave your family and children; you leave your wife.
You travel many miles; you go where you're told,
in any weather, whether hot or cold.
You don't want to go; you'd rather stay home,
but you go anyway, from your family you're alone.
You're thought of by everyone here in the States,
please come home soon, you're missed, make haste.
I thank you for your sacrifice, your courage, your time,
I thank you for your commitment; to me you're sublime.
Thank you for your commitment that will never part,
this thank you is from the bottom of my heart.

Freedom

Thank you for giving us our freedom,
thank you for saving us from all heathens.
Because of your unselfishness we are free,
to choose how to live, the future we can see.
There's not enough we can do to show gratitude,
but those we lost, our Father made room.
You gave us freedom and love from afar,
you didn't even know who we are.
You stayed with it until victory was ours,
and we know our Father gave you that power.
You fought so hard and gave us your love,
the perfect example of that power from above.
Thank you again for your humble devotion,
thank you again for stilling that commotion.

Dedicated to all those who gave their lives for world freedom.

Personal Feelings

From a young age, and even now, expressing my feelings has been challenging. I believe that God used poems, such as the ones in this section, as an outlet of expression for me. As world situations unfolded, or extremely personal happenings affected my everyday life, I would turn to poetry to record my positive or negative thoughts. That gave me the ability to think before I reacted. God seemed to place words in my mind that were destined to be recorded into these poems to record my own lessons learned, and also to possibly offer a pathway for others who read them. If these ponderings help anyone from causing harm to another or making decisions based on emotion instead of wisdom, then the effort to record them was certainly worthwhile.

"Keep on loving one another as brothers and sisters."
Hebrews 13:1

"May God arise, may his enemies be scattered;
may his foes flee before him."
Psalms 68:1

These Poems

Because of You, Father, these poems have come about,
only You could have written them, I have no doubt.
You gave me the words, and I wrote them down,
but we need to finish keeping them around.
So give me the words, Your will to do,
and we'll put it together and show your love, too.
We'll spread Your Word throughout the world,
the trees will sing, the rocks will twirl.
These short poems are to honor You this day,
both You, dear Lord, and God the same way.
To praise and glorify your Holy names
is the purpose of these poems, they are all the same.

Where Do I Go

What do I do Father, where do I go?
it is so overwhelming; I just don't know.
I need your wisdom, I need your help,
I can't decide all by myself.
So tell me, Father, what do I do?
I don't want to make myself look like a fool.
You are the Almighty, You know it all,
help me decide, don't let me fall.

Where Am I Going?

Where am I going, how do I get through?
Who do I see, what do I do?
Then it hits me like a brick. Don't you know?
My Lord is with me. He'll never let go.
He loves me forever in so many ways,
during the darkest of nights and the brightest of days.
Thank you, Lord, for never letting go,
for You know, I too, love you so.
Thank you for being there and showing me the way,
thank you for being with me day after day.
Thank You, Lord, so very much,
thank You, Lord, for staying in touch.

Domestic Violence

Domestic violence is a tragic end,
we need to fight it, we need to defend.
The helpless ones who it truly hurts
need our help to assert.
How could they do this to God's people?
How could they treat life so feeble?
It's bad enough accidents take people's lives,
but to do it on purpose is a crime, that's no lie.
So support these people with your love,
let them know it comes from above.

Kids Are Crying

Kids are crying,
kids are dying.
Kids feel alone,
they feel like cold stone.
No matter where you go upon this earth,
there are kids who really hurt.
We're put down here to show God's love,
instead we're keeping them from their home above.
We need to do what God wants us to,
we need to show love, how about you?
So let's stop crying and let's stop dying,
show these kids love and stop their crying.
No matter how hard it is or how long it takes,
all of our futures are at stake.
Stop thinking about ourselves and show God's love,
we all want to go to our home up above.

Pain

At times, pain overrides friendship by far,
and the outcome is I become very hard.
People don't matter and neither does life,
for all you do is live in strive.
You work your nails to the bone,
and you still end up living alone.
But stop for a minute and take a time-out.
God is always with you, there is no doubt.

Cut Down

Cut down in the prime of his life,
leaving behind his child and his wife.
Where is the justice in that senseless murder?
Now his family has to overcome that hurdle.
Over some stupid argument not worth to mention,
it's so far beyond comprehension.
What right does anyone have to take another's life,
leaving behind his child and his wife?
A senseless act that one could avoid,
now an innocent family is destroyed.
Where is his daddy to celebrate his birthday?
Where is his daddy to wake him on Christmas Day?
Where is his daddy to teach him baseball?
Where is his daddy to teach him football?
With a little common sense and self-control,
this family would have a full household.
Hopefully in the future people will stop and think,
and an innocent family will not, by one, shrink.
So, the bottom line is—think before you act,
that is the most important and simple fact.
Don't lose your temper, don't lose your cool,
everyone will be safe, and you won't be a fool.

Three Time Loser

You know Lord; I've been a loser all my life,
you know Lord; I've been a loser right from the start.
I lost my mother to the first breath of air
that's the way my life has been.
I lost my wife to the drugs that I've done,
I lost my second wife to alcohol.
The third one's got to be from my heart, Lord,
so, it'll grow from now on, day by day.
So, I sit here at the bar room,
looking at my glass of wine.
Looking at the reflections of my life,
then I see just what my life has been like, Lord.
And I don't want any part of it now.
I don't want to be a three-time loser,
I don't want to be a broken man.
I don't want to be a three-time loser,
So, Lord won't you show me if you can.
I don't want to be a three-time loser,
I don't want to be a broken man.
I don't want to be a three-time loser,
so, Lord won't you show me the way.
I don't want to be a three-time loser,
so, Lord show me the way.

Written by my brother, James Harris

Happy Birthday, America

Happy Birthday, America, you've come a long way,
from thirteen new colonies, you fought hard to stay.
From the very beginning you wanted to be free,
and you really are, can't you see?
Though at times you wonder if you really are,
from what could have been you've really come far.
You'll always have a bully who will give you doubts,
but with hope and faith, it'll come about.
There'll always be Someone who is watching over you,
just keep the faith, and you will get through.
So Happy Birthday, America, enjoy your day,
May you always remember how you arrived that way.

Happy Birthday

On this warm and spring-like day,
a Happy Birthday comes your way.
And with a wish for many more,
of health and happiness, you will only soar.
So enjoy this day, you deserve it well.
This is your day, so ring the bell.
We're all here to celebrate this day,
Enjoy the love, it's here to stay.

Michael Jackson

Gone from this life, the King of Pop,
but your music goes on, it will never stop.
Your life was tough, but you saw it through,
you were only human, as we are, too.
May God forgive your way of life,
may He see your help in others' strife.
We're on this earth for a few short years;
we laugh many laughs and cry many tears.
We couldn't understand some of the things you did,
but only God could see where you hid.
You were misunderstood and criticized,
now may all your good be realized.
Goodbye, dear friend. You'll be missed a great deal,
may all that you started continue to heal.
Forgive him, Father, forgive him now,
open your arms, him into your house allow.

Listen My Children

Listen my children and listen well,
there is something that I must tell.
There's no reason to hurt, no reason to cry,
someone will listen, that's no lie.
You will feel better without a doubt,
talk to someone, just let it out.
Letting it out may cause some hurt,
but believe me you won't feel like dirt.
Let out your hurt, let out your pain.
Life is much better without the strain.
Share your problem, share your grief,
tell your parents, you'll find relief.
There's always someone ready to hear,
just talk things over, there's nothing to fear.
Don't criticize yourself about any mistake,
talk to someone before it's too late.

Where Did I Go Wrong?

Where did I go wrong to deserve this?
What did I do, what did I miss?
All I ever wanted was compassion and love,
to enjoy life from the ground or above.
To work together and to create
is such a fulfilling feeling (joy), that must be great.
But unfortunately, each day we grow further apart,
how do we end this, where do we start?
All I ever did was try to do what's right,
at what point did I lose the sight?

I Want Her Back

Just as Christ forgave us and wanted us back,
I forgive you and want the same just like that.
Oh Lord, now I know how you must have felt!
You know how much I need Your help!
Open her eyes and open her heart,
let her see we should never part.

I'm So Lonesome

I'm so lonesome I could cry,
I love you so much, and that's no lie.
I want you to stop and meditate,
my feelings for you just can't wait.
My love for you runs so deep,
I finally realize it is you I seek.
I hear your voice every day,
I hear your voice in every way.
The loves I had never seemed real,
but my love for you is the real deal.
I see you in my mind in everything I do,
I see your image every day, and night, too.
When I go to sleep I think of you,
when I wake up, I wish you were there, too.
I hurt inside when you're not around,
my heart longs to hear your sound.
My heart aches, so great is the pain,
my love is so deep, I can't explain.
My only wish is to grow old with you,
I love you so much, I truly do.
Please, dear God, help us to be,
together forever, the only way to be.

You Broke My Heart

Oh baby, my love, you broke my heart
when you told me you wanted to part.
What did I do that you wanted to leave?
How can I make you understand and believe?
I love you, love you so much,
I don't want to lose you or lose your touch.
How can I keep you from going away?
What can I do to make you stay?
Please tell me, tell me now,
let me know, tell me how
To keep you from feeling this way.
I don't want you to go, please, I pray.
So tell me, what can I do?
How can I stop being such a fool?
Why won't you believe me when I say
I love you so much in every way?
So tell me, tell me what to do.
How can we stay together, stay as two?

Memories

Memories are printed on my mind,
the life we've shared was as sweet as wine.
The first time I saw you, I wanted you for life,
that's why I married you and made you my wife.
I knew I wanted you to be my spouse,
I wanted to take care of you and our house.

Broken Dreams

At one time you were the love of my life,
and that is when you became my wife.
But we had differences, and you broke my heart,
and it was evident we had to part.
It was hard to do, but it was right,
and we both continued on with life.
Now God has taken you home with Him
to a place we have never been.
Don't be afraid, go in peace,
no more pain to say the least.
Just know that from the start,
you will always have a place in my heart.

Praising God

As with many of the words that flow from my pen, they often became a praise or a lamentation, depending on the inspiration. God always had a plan about where my words would land, in the same way that He has a plan for the lives of each one of us. Though my walk through life was not that of a poet, at least for my profession, I am living proof that God works through even Shop and Broadcasting teachers to spread His Word. I sincerely hope some of these thoughts touch each of you, causing a momentary pause.

Many times, we do not take the time to stop and thank God for the many blessings He continues to give us, even when we do not deserve it. Our lives might be very different if our Father had decided to give up on us. His grace and mercy for us endures forever, no matter what challenges are laid before us, either from our Lord as He shapes and molds us, or as a result of our own unwise choices. As the song lyric proclaims: "Praise God from whom all blessings flow."

"Sing to the Lord, all you godly ones! Praise His holy name."
Psalm 30:4

"Let the godly sing for joy to the Lord;
it is fitting for the pure to praise Him."
Psalms 33:1

"For the word of the Lord holds true,
and we can trust everything He does."
Psalms 33:4

Save Our Soul

He came into this world to save our soul,
resurrection, you know, was His goal.
His life was full of turmoil and pain,
many a day it was a strain.
We don't deserve His patience and time,
we're too busy hurting and doing the crime.
Despite our arrogance He came down,
for the first time, light shone all around.
His eyes on our Father, He got through it,
and now His light is always lit.
Thank You, Lord Jesus, for your love,
not only from You but also from above.
Thank You, Father, for Your love so true,
thank You, Father, for being our glue.
You hold onto us when the times get rough,
that's the only way we can stay so tough.
Thank You, Father, for a brand-new start,
and with Your help, we'll never part.

Thank You, Lord

Thank you, God, for my health,
thank you, God, for your help.
Thank you, God, for time and space,
for helping me run this race.
This world is heartless every day,
but with you there's always a way
To get away from the greed and dope,
and look up to see there's hope.
Give me patience, give me faith,
help me win this tiring race.

The Desert

Into the desert you went,
until Your strength was spent.
Like a rock, You resisted
what Satan strongly insisted.
On the cross, the victory You won
because You are our Father's Son.
You took our sins as Your own
so that one day we could go home.
Thank You, Lord Jesus, for saving our souls,
thank You, Lord Jesus, for being so bold.
Thank You for beating corruption,
for giving us hope and satisfaction.
You are the One, You are the Son,
You are the One, the victory won.
You finished what our Father willed You to do,
help us to be just like You.

Thank You For Waiting

Thank You, Father, for waiting for me,
thank You, Father, for hoping I'd see.
Forgive me, Father, for being so defiant,
forgive me, Father, for being so uncompliant.
I thought I knew everything in life,
but all I did was increase my strife.
I didn't listen, I didn't care,
I forgot You'd be with me everywhere.
I wanted to do it my way and enjoy this world,
all I did was send my head spinning in such a swirl.
I forgot You told me You'd never let go,
it was hard to understand how You love me so.
I don't deserve Your unselfish love
that flows down every day from above.
So thank You, Father, for waiting for me,
thank you, Father, for helping me see.

Thank You, Father

You brought me into this world loved only by you,
this world that was so hard and so cruel.
You stayed with me no matter what I did,
at times I wondered how I would live.
You gave me a chance in this hard life.
You taught me how to survive this strife.
With your loving and caring tones,
for my entire life I wasn't alone.
You taught me how to love each other,
how to care and help one another.
When I'm in pain You're always there,
when I need advice, You're always fair.
Thank You for Your love, thank You for Your life,
thank You for carrying me through all this strife.
Your wisdom always pointed me the way,
it kept me from slipping or going astray.
You knew what You were doing when You gave me life,
You knew what I needed, even through any strife.
I love you more than I can say,
I love you more as each day slips away.
Thank you for giving me life when you did,
thank you for never giving up on this kid.

Holy Spirit, Live Within Me

Come Holy Spirit, live within me,
clean up my life and let me see.
Come, Holy Spirit, into my heart,
come, Holy Spirit, let's not part.
My Father's love that will set me free
from the troubles of this world that has a grip on me.
Help me to see what my Father wills,
keep me on track and keep me still.
Don't let me slip, don't let me fall,
help me to see my Father's call.
Give me courage to obey my Father,
give me strength to follow like no other.
Come, Holy Spirit, hold on to me,
come, Holy Spirit, and help me see.
Thank You, Lord Jesus, for saving my soul,
thank You, Lord Jesus, for making me whole.
Thank You, Father, for Your love from above,
continue to ascend on me like the Holy dove.
Thank You, Holy Spirit, for keeping me safe,
continue to stay with me, please make haste.
I want You with me wherever I go,
I desperately need You, don't let me go.

God Is So Wonderful

My God, thou art so wonderful,
my God thou art so powerful.
You give me strength in any strife,
You help me through this hard-struggling life.
Sometimes it's difficult to know what's true,
and sometimes the only one to turn to is You.
Other times You direct me to friends like mine,
and they help me feel so good, so fine.
I'm the wealthiest person on this earth,
You had it figured before my birth.
I love you dearly for that chance,
I could just jump up and begin to dance.
I hope to have them for the rest of my life,
through thick and thin through any strife.
For if you have true friends like that,
you'll always succeed when you're at bat.

I Love You, Lord

I love you, Lord, with all my heart,
I pray each day that we never part.
I need you, Lord, every day,
in this day it's so easy to stray.
You're so merciful and understanding,
for you, Lord, are always bending.
My patience is so narrow, so thin,
but you always ask where I've been.
You're so wise and so strong,
to you I'll always want to belong.

Jesus

Jesus, Jesus, Jesus, the greatest name I know,
just tell me what to do, just tell me where to go.
To say Your name is powerful and right,
darkness is gone, replaced by light.
Your love is so strong, it draws me to You,
Your love is so strong, I just want to be with You.
I know my love can never match Yours,
but I keep trying and can only accept Yours.
I know you see my limitations and understand,
I know my life You've already planned.
I won't stop trying to improve my all,
I hope by doing so I will have answered your call.

Jesus, Be Our Guest

Come, Lord Jesus, be our guest,
make our home the very best.
Teach me Your will, I'll keep them to the end,
I'll obey Your word, I'll never bend.
I'll put them into practice with all my heart,
for that is where my happiness starts.
I find my joy in all Your commands,
help me to always, forever, understand.
All of our lives are in your hands,
all across this wonderful land.
The Lord is for me, I will have no fear,
with that promise, He's always near.

You Gave Me Life

You gave me life when no one else would,
You gave me life when no one else could.
If it wasn't for You, where else would I be,
if it wasn't for You, no one else would see.
You taught me the meaning of real true love,
You showed me the love that comes from above.
Thank you, Lord Jesus, for being so loving,
thank you, Lord Jesus, for being so giving.

I'll Love My God

I'll love my God always,
now and until the end of my days.
And if I continue to love him so much,
I'll not worry He'll keep in touch.
For my days are numbered but won't end at death,
because in heaven I'll receive new breath.
And I'll praise my God for all my years,
even though I may shed some tears.
Because of that man of glory,
I can tell that old, old story
of the birth and death of Jesus Christ.
Our dear Lord paid our price.
So, at this trying time of life,
through the calm and through the strife.
Get down on your knees and pray
for patience and guidance throughout the day.
For you, dear God, we'll try to be
faithful and true for eternity.

O Lord

O Lord, I love you so much,
I know you'll always stay in touch.
I may do wrong and do sinful things,
but to you I'll release everything.
You'll always stay in my heart,
and for eternity we'll never part.
Even though I may go astray,
I'm still with you day by day.
So give me the strength to live each hour,
and let me feel thy Holy Power.

Lord, I'll Always Love You

I'll always love you, Lord, no matter what I think,
allow me the pleasure of your love to drink.
Take away the confusion, take away the fear,
help me to know that you're always near.
Help me feel your presence, let me hear you,
let me know you're there, let me know it's true.
Allow me to sleep, let me rest,
I know you're always here, I don't have to guess.
I seek your wisdom, I seek your love,
I seek your strength and Spirit from above.

Be More Like God

(Reverie)
Why, dear God, can't we be more like you?
Why, dear God, can't we always be true?
Why do we try to do everything our way?
Why is it so easy to stray?
Why does sin seem so easy and fun?
Why does darkness cover our sun?
Your right hand, O Lord, is majestic in power,
it covers us all hour after hour.
It's always there during our worst of times,
help us to look ahead and never behind.
Help us to understand your will,
make our hearts and minds be still.

Magnificent God

O God, You are so magnificent,
Your love is so resplendent.
Earth is Your footstool, and Heaven is Your throne,
glory to raise,
Your Heaven is full of Your splendor,
Your earth is full of Your praise.
Let the heavens be glad, let the earth celebrate,
let the seas and fields exult
and all that is in it not hesitate.
All the trees will sing for joy before Your presence,
may I, too, join the chorus in my penitence.
Thank You for your magnificent wonders and ways,
with hope I will follow and never stray.
With one arm You rule with strength and might,
with the other You gather me close
and keep me in sight.
Hear me, magnificent God,
I love you with all my heart,
I pray for Your strength
and love that we will never part.

I Think Of You, Lord

When I look up into the air,
and see birds flying everywhere,
I think of you, Lord.
When I look out over the sea,
and see the fish swimming free,
I think of you, Lord.
When I stare at the trees and flowers,
and think to myself, hour after hour,
I think of you, Lord.
When I go for a walk and hear the sounds,
and breathe the oxygen that's all around,
I think of you, Lord.
When I look at the cross on Calvary,
why are they so mad, this society?
I think of you, Lord.
When I hear about these people on dope,
and they complain about there's no hope,
I think of you, Lord.
When I feel other people interfering with my life,
stealing what I have and giving me constant strife,
I think of you, Lord.
When I look at my family and friends,
then onto my knees I quickly bend,
I think of you, Lord.
And thank you for these people in my life,
even with all the sorrows and the strife.
We look to you for strength and faith,
and hope to survive this human race.
I'll always think of you, Lord.

Easter Morning

On this blessed and glorious day,
our Lord and Savior showed us the way.
He loved us so much He gave us His life,
we were so blind we couldn't see the light.
He promised to save us from ourselves and foes,
in which direction to go we did not know.
He made a promise not to let go,
He obeyed our Father, shouldn't we also?
To bring us into the family, He knew He had to die,
but at the same time, in three days He'd be alive.
So let's rejoice and sing His song,
for in His family we all belong.
Just believe in the life of Jesus Christ,
He'll take care of us for the rest of our life.

Happy Father's Day

My Father of all fathers,
You gave me Christ, my savior and brother.
Because of You, I have a place in your house,
in my heart I have no doubt.
You knew me before I was born,
You never wavered, especially when I was scorned.
You gave me hope and my faith,
To be with You I can hardly wait.
on this day we celebrate Father's Day,
But with You, every day we should always say:
Happy Father's Day.

We celebrate our fathers in this world. But do we take
one second to wish our Heavenly Father a Happy Fa-
ther's Day? So, in recognition of our Heavenly Father,
I dedicate this poem.

God Speaking

The poems in this section were created by my deep-rooted anger toward unkind people and the acts they perform. To tolerate my total distaste for bullying, bigotry, lies, hatred, indifference, etc., I imagined how God might express Himself when faced with these attitudes and manipulations, and the pain they cause others. Yes, I believe that God feels pain caused by His children. When we destroy the amazingly beautiful world that he created, and destroy each other, God weeps. Obviously, I am not God, nor could I begin to understand the awesome depth, width, and breadth of His purity of love, even in the midst of these appalling moral flaws.

Writing these poems gave me an outlet for my anger, and a place for me to unload my disappointments, pain, and disgust brought on by everyday occurrences or encounters.

"The Lord gives righteousness and justice to
all who are treated unfairly."
Psalm 103:6

"I lavish unfailing love to a thousand generations. I forgive iniquity,
rebellion, and sin. But I do not excuse the guilty! I lay the sins of
the parents upon their children and grandchildren; the entire family is
affected—even children in the third and fourth generations."
Exodus 34:7

Why Won't You Understand

What's the matter with you people, don't you understand?
it is the same all over, throughout this land.
I put you on this earth to help each other,
but instead, you go against one another.
What will it take to make you see it my way?
You could have many more blessings every day.
I even sent my son to help you see,
but you put Him on the cross to save your greed.
People are hurting and dying everywhere,
why won't you follow Me, don't you care?
Do unto others as you would have them do unto you,
and with you I'll always be true.
Start helping each other and pave the way,
be faithful and strong and never stray.
My love for you is strong and true,
I open my arms to welcome you.

Listen Man

I love you, man, why don't you listen to me?
I'm trying to help you, don't you see?
You're hurting yourself and those who love you,
if you don't take care of yourself, it's all over for you.
So, Listen to Me and listen well,
then you will know, and you can tell.
Stop hurting yourself and your loved ones, too,
and all will know and come back to you.

My World

This is My world and you are My people,
nothing and no one can take you from Me.
Just believe in Me and I'll set you free,
no sickness or war can keep you from Me.
I cannot be defeated so believe that's true,
so don't worry or fret, My Son and I are here for you.

I Am Your Father

I am your Father, why all this violence?
I made you all the same with some common sense.
Just open your eyes and see My light,
no reason to argue, aggravate, or fight.
I put you on this earth to help each other,
sometimes I wonder why I even bothered.
I put you here to take care of my world,
but what I see makes my head swirl.
Start treating each other with proper respect,
otherwise you better drop and hit the deck.
There will be a time when I will have enough,
and as the Israelites saw, you will feel My stuff.
So, hear me well and listen to Me,
repent of your actions and I'll set you free.
I love you so much, I truly do,
hear Me and come back to Me, won't you?

Frustration

What's the matter with you people, are you so blind?
I've given My life for you, if you don't mind.
Why won't you follow Me and hear what I say?
Why won't you open your eyes when I lead the way?
All you have to do is listen, and I'll tell you what to do,
just listen and your life will prosper for you.
I promise you, I won't lead you astray,
I will guide you every step of the way.
Don't be afraid or discouraged, just follow Me,
I promise you, you will feel free.
You will have peace of mind like a gentle breeze,
ask Me and I'll put you at ease.
So listen to what I have to say,
and have your life be brighter every day.

*"What I really liked is how the mood switched from harsh
to desperation because "all you have to do...I won't lead you
astray...I'll guide you every step of the way..." Also, a theolog-
ical note in this poem, there is a true freedom we have when we
listen and follow."*
--Pastor Jason Caddy, Lead Pastor, Grace Church of
the Nazarene, Columbia, TN.

Have Courage

Have courage and be brave,
you made a mistake, now you must pay.
But I'll be with you to the very end,
giving you strength and hope and always a friend.
Remember my promise, I'll be with you always,
every second, every hour of every day.
So when it gets tough, and you think you can't make it,
remember your friend, my cross,
and how you must bear it.
Your friends will be waiting for you to come home,
we'll always be there, and you won't be alone.

I Made You

I made you, I gave you life,
why do you refuse to see My light?
Why do you insist on living on your own?
Your problems cause you to be alone.
Invite Me in and let Me help you,
your life will be better once you do.
I love you and want to help you see,
listen to Me and please believe.
I want the best for you and enrich your life,
I will help you relieve all strife.
So let me in and let's live together,
and let's see how your life is better.

Hope

There is always hope, there is always a path,
though things seem impossible, that will never last.
For I am possible, even though you are not,
I will always be with you, I will never stop.
I am the way, you'll never be alone,
never try to make it on your own.
You are never lost when you cling to Me,
with Me by your side, you'll always feel free.
You are not lost when you remember you're found,
you are never lost when I'm around.
When mistakes are made, don't look for a solution without Me,
I will help you, I am the way, don't you see!
I have come, I am the one with the plan,
with all the pain I will help you withstand.
Do you know what the plan always involves from above?
No matter what has happened, or what is said:
you are always LOVED!

Why This Violence?

I'm your Father, why all this violence?
I made you all the same with common sense.
Just open your eyes and see My light,
no reason to argue, bully, or fight.
I put you here to help each other,
sometimes I wonder why I bothered.
I put you here to take care of my world,
but what I see makes My head swirl.
Start treating each other with proper respect,
all you're doing is making My world a wreck.
There'll be a time when I'll have enough,
as the Israelites saw, you'll feel My stuff.
So hear Me loud and listen to Me,
repent of your sins and I'll set you free.
I love you so much, I truly do,
listen to Me and let Me come back to you.
Never forget, I'm always with you,
whenever you're happy, whenever you're blue.
Even though you may forget Me,
I'm always with you, just wait and see.
I will never leave you no matter what,
to you that's a promise and that is that.

Bible
Characters

As I read the books of the Old Testament, it seemed as if God spoke to me. I began to arrange the thoughts I was having into a poem. So that none were lost, I immediately wrote the words as I received them. I imagined what life was like for each character, putting myself in their place, feeling the joys and pains of their hearts. These were the worst of times, and only God could deliver the characters from the enemy that was always swirling around. Although each challenge was different, God brought them through every storm, offering a new beginning and blessings beyond every expectation. If we open our hearts to God, and replicate the faithfulness of these characters, our God will shower us with many blessings as well.

"For the Lord watches over the path of the godly,
but the path of the wicked leads to destruction."
Psalm 1:6

"It was by faith that the people of Israel went right through the Red Sea as though they were on dry ground. But when the Egyptians tried to follow, they were all drowned."
Hebrews 11:29

To King Nebuchadnezzar

O Nebuchadnezzar, we do not need to defend ourselves,
for the story we have, to all the world we tell.
If we are thrown into the blazing furnace,
the God we serve is able to save us in earnest.
But even if He does not, we want you to know,
we will not serve your gods or your images of gold.
So do what you must to save your face,
for we will never fall from our God's grace.
But if you want what we talk about,
just listen to us as we shout.
For you, too, can have God's love,
just open your heart and receive it from above.

From King Nebuchadnezzar

I've had a dream that troubles me so,
tell me what it means, I want to know.
This is what will happen, you will soon have seen,
if you don't tell me about it or what it means.
I will have you cut into pieces and your houses into rubble,
there won't be anything left of you,
not even a stubble.
But if you tell me the dream and you explain,
there will be no sorrow or even pain.
You will receive from me gifts and rewards of great honor,
so tell me the dreams, don't let me ponder.

Noah's Ark

Outside surrounded by water and weather fair,
inside many animals in pairs.
How did we get into this predicament?
no solid ground to pitch a tent.
Depending on you, Lord, for all our needs,
still searching and searching for that grass to feed.
We know you'll bring all of us through
despite this punishment for disobeying You.
We patiently wait for sight of land
to continue to live for what you have planned.
So hear our cries, and hear our prayers,
take care of us and all our cares.
Thank you, Lord, for choosing us,
thank you, Lord, for in you we trust.

Satan

Well, Satan, you thought you'd get away
with the crime,
you of all should realize, you'll do the time.
You thought you'd get all of us to follow you,
but the power of God would continue
through and through.
No one can resist the will of God, not even you,
it's more powerful than anything, you know that's true.
So accept the fact that you will never win,
for God has the power over all our sin.
Now crawl into your hole and never come out,
for now what you can do is like a child pout.

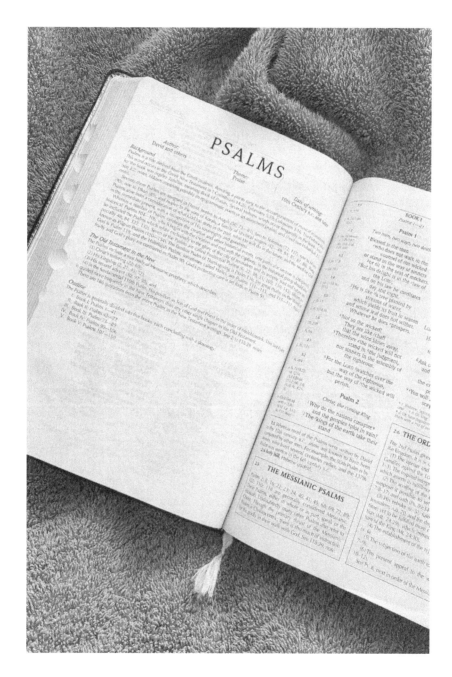

PSALMS

Author: David and others

Theme: Praise

Date of writing: 10th Century B.C. and was

The Old Testament in the New

Outline

Psalm 1

Psalm 2

Christ, the coming King

THE MESSIANIC PSALMS

BOOK 1

THE ORD...

Psalms

"Yea, though I walk through the valley of the shadow of death, I shall fear no evil, for thou art with me...." I can only imagine how David was feeling as he hunkered down, surrounded by his enemies. Most great warriors would have been strategizing a battle plan, bolstering his men, and sizing up the enemy's encampments, relying solely on the strength of his fighters. Instead, Psalm 23 showed how peaceful and confident David was that the Lord would hold him closely through all circumstances, even in death.

For many years, I have found comfort in the Psalms. Their stories, many written by King David, seem very close to my own experiences. The words that emerged in my head became a form of expression tying my joy, pain, frustration or sorrow to the psalmist as I read. I hope these words will offer meaning that extends a lifeline to all who read them.

"Blessed is the man who does not walk in the counsel of the wicked or stand in the way of sinners or sit in the seat of mockers."
Psalm 1:1

"For the Lord watches over the way of the righteous, but the way of the wicked will perish."
Psalm 1:6

Psalm 44
Rise O Lord

Awake, O Lord, are You asleep?
rouse Yourself, from us, don't keep.
Why do you hide and forget our misery?
You've always been there throughout history.
We're brought down to the dust of the ground,
rise up and help us, for Your love is sound.
We face death all day long,
yet we try to forget through your songs.
So rise up, Lord, and be with us,
for it is Your love we truly trust.

Psalm 51

Have mercy on me, O God,
because of your unfailing love,
let it descend like rain from above.
Because of your great compassion,
blot out the stain of my sins,
wash me clean from my guilt, purify me from within.
I recognize my rebellion; it haunts me day and night,
against You and You alone I have sinned
and done evil in your sight.
So have mercy on me, O God,
and help me do what is right,
hold me in your arms, don't let go,
and squeeze me ever so tight.

Psalm 63

O God You're my God; I earnestly search for You,
for You my soul thirsts, and my body longs, that's true.
In a dry and weary land where there is no water,
somehow, some way, there always seems some order.
I have seen You in the sanctuary and beheld Your
power and glory,
Your love is better than life;
my lips will always tell Your story.
I will praise You as long as I exist,
and Your name will always come from my lips.
My soul will be satisfied as with the richest of foods,
with grateful heart, I will always praise you through
and through.
On my bed, I remember You
and thank You through the night,
because You are my help, I will sing in the shadows of
Your wings and in the light.
My soul will always cling tightly to You,
Your right hand holds me up no matter what I do.
In the shadow of Your wings I sing for joy,
my soul clings to You, keep me close, I implore.

Psalm 125

Those who trust in the Lord are like Mount Zion,
it cannot be shaken and stands like a lion.
As the mountains surround Jerusalem
for miles around,
so the Lord, his people,
both now and forevermore, surrounds.
The scepter of the wicked will not remain
over the land allotted to the righteous to sustain.
For then the righteous in their foolishness might use
their hands to do evil against mankind, that's true.
Do good, O Lord, to those who are good,
to those who are upright in heart, feed them your
righteous food.
But those who turn to crooked ways
the Lord will banish with the evildoers,
and those who stray.
Peace be upon Israel.

Psalm 130

I wait for the Lord, my soul waits,
I wait for the Lord, He doesn't hesitate.
In His word is my hope,
with His word, this life I cope.
My soul waits for the Lord every hour,
I know in my heart He has all the power.
For with the Lord there's steadfast love,
my Lord has sent this down from above.
And with Him there is plenty of redemption,
and soon He will take us into His dimension.

Christmas

The Christmas story in the Book of Matthew describes a challenging time for all concerned. As I read, my pen began to flow with the emotion each person may have felt. Although we view Christmas as a time of joy, all those involved experienced differing levels of joy, understanding, faithfulness, and compassion. These people were experiencing a very special time in their lives, orchestrated by God in order to bring our Savior Jesus into the world. Yet, God was ever so faithful to carry them through. The joy often became confusing, and they did not know what to expect with each step. But they still pushed forward and did what they were told.

As I reflect on their journey, I hope that, if God called me to such a difficult but rewarding challenge, that I would answer with the faithfulness that they did.

"But the angel reassured them. "Don't be afraid!" he said. "I bring great joy to all people. The Savior---yes, the Messiah, the Lord---has been born today in Bethlehem, the city of David."
Luke 2:10-11

Mary

My soul glorifies the Lord and rejoices in God, my Savior,
He has been mindful of his servant's humble behavior.
From now on all generations will call me blessed,
for my Father has done great things for me—
I must have passed the test.
His mercy extends to those who love Him,
From generation to generation is where it's been.
He has performed mighty deeds with His arms;
scattered those proud in their thoughts and caused harm.
He has brought down rulers from their thrones,
lifted up the humble and brought them home.
He has filled the hungry with good things,
but sent the rich away empty, as well as kings.
He has helped His servant, Israel,
remembering to be merciful, but harshly to deal.
To Abraham and his descendants forever,
even as He said to our fathers: always endeavor.

Inn Keeper

What can I do, how can I serve?
I'm quite busy, if you haven't heard.
I'm so busy since the decree came out,
I can't hear you, you have to shout.
You see how crowded it is, there is no room,
I hope this census is over soon.
If it is a room you want, sorry to say,
to squeeze you in there's just no way.
I wish I had a place for you to lie down,
but as you can see I'm full, just look around.
It'll take a week to get these people out of here,
if you can wait, I'll see what I can do, have no fear.
But if you can't wait and need a place to rest,
there's a manger out back, there's none the best.
So make yourself at home and lie awhile,
don't worry about the place. There is no style.

Shepherd's Song

Let's go see what the Angel talked about,
let's go see, so there is no doubt.
He says this event is close to where we are,
that's good for us; we can't go far.
The sheep will be fine where they lay,
where the grass is they will stay.
So let us hurry and see this sight,
then we'll be back by morning's light.

The Magi

Where is the one who has been born king of the Jews?
We saw His star in the east
and have come to worship him, too.
We've come a great distance by following his star,
our home is not around here, it is quite far.
We want to see Him before we go home,
we don't want to miss this; we want to be shown.
So tell us quickly, we don't want to delay,
tell us the direction, tell us the way.
So tell us now. We have gifts for Him,
tell us where we can find the forgiver of sins.

Star So Wonderous

Star so wonderous, star so bright,
the brightest star I see tonight.
Why do you shine so bright today?
Why do I see you during the day?
You shine so much brighter than all the rest,
your light outshines even the best.
Why do you shine all night and day?
It seems you're trying to show me the way.
Where am I going? I don't know,
but I will follow you wherever you go.
Where will you go? Where will you rest?
Are you putting me through some kind of test?
It doesn't matter, I don't care,
I will follow you everywhere.

How I Love Christmas

This Christmas is so special to me
because I'm celebrating it with thee.
Not only the gift giving, but the nativity, too,
who else would celebrate it this way but you?
It's great to celebrate Christ's birth
with the nicest person on this earth.
So Merry Christmas and a Happy New Year.
I hope I can bring you lots of good cheer.

All I Want For Christmas

All I want for Christmas is you,
and I hope that is what you want, too.
My love grows stronger as each day goes by,
but with the holidays even more so, and it never dies.
So don't worry about gifts; I already have you,
all I need for Christmas is you.

Happy Birthday Jesus

Happy Birthday, Jesus Christ,
thank you for our brand-new life.
We celebrate your day with our love,
our love that's given to us from above.
You didn't have to risk your life,
you didn't have to live that strife,
But you did to show your love to us,
and for that we thank you so very much.
Thank you, God, for your Son,
thank you, God, from everyone.
Happy Birthday, Jesus Christ,
with many more throughout my life.

THROUGH THEIR EYES

EASTER MUSICAL

Words by George F. Harris Jr. and Andrea C. Harris
Music by Andrea C. Harris and Buddy Skipper
Arranged by Buddy Skipper

Through Their Eyes

As my poems began to accumulate, I realized that several of them seemed to speak directly from the voices of Jesus' disciples. I decided to compile several of these poems into a screenplay, but it seemed to lack the emotional depth and excitement typically needed to hold an audience. Transforming the poems into songs seemed the best solution. But how?

I was not a musician or songwriter, but God directed me to a woman in my church who was not only a composer in her own right, but came from a family of musicians and a music arranger. After many recording sessions in Nashville, nineteen of my poems became songs for a Contemporary Christian musical entitled *Through Their Eyes*. That was also the creation of Windfalls Productions (a name suggested by my late father). Even better, the woman from church later became my lovely wife!

In 2016, the longer version containing mostly vocal solos was reproduced into a choir version (cantata). Both versions, as well as other anthems, are available at www.windfallsproductions.com. You can also read a brief summary of our story, as well as find other anthems we have written. We have been commissioned to spread God's word and love, and He gives us the skills and wisdom to do just that. Ask for His help, and see what you can accomplish!

Praise God through whom all blessings flow!

"Therefore, go and make disciples of all the nations, baptizing them in the name of the Father and the Son and the Holy Spirit. Teach these new disciples to obey all the commands I have given you. And be sure of this: I am with you always, even to the end of the age."
Matthew 28:19-20

Being Weak

Please forgive me, Lord for being so weak,
and help me find You, for it's You whom I seek.
I know at this time it's hard to see,
I truly love You, You're the one for me.
Take me with You, let me follow Your life,
allow me the Kingdom, You are my light.
I love you Lord, truly I do,
I always, forever, want to be with You.

Doubting Your Word

Forgive me, Lord, for doubting Your word,
forgive me, Lord, for not believing what I've heard.
Jesus, our Lord, has risen today,
Jesus, our Lord, has shown us the way.
He's shown us how we are to serve,
and to have faith on what we have heard.
Thank you, Jesus, for Your life,
for showing us how to deal with strife.
You have shown us how to take care of each other,
You have given us love that is unlike any other.
Even though I have doubts at times,
I still believe that I'm Yours and You're mine.
I truly love You, Lord, yes, I do,
I can't wait until I'm living with You.
Thank You, Jesus, for Your fight,
thank You, Jesus, for Your life.
I trust You, Jesus, with all my heart,
I trust You, Jesus, that we'll never part.

Fishin'

Father, we're working as fast as we can,
there's a lot of net here, don't you understand?
Wasn't there another business you could start?
Why did you take this one to heart?
This job is so long and hard to do,
normally, we would follow you anywhere, that's true.
So just have patience and give us a break,
and soon we all will be out on the lake.
The days are so long and at times so hot,
and some days we can't even fill the pot.
Some days I don't even feel like fishing,
Please, father, won't you just listen?
Won't you help us, give us a hand?
Then we will finish sooner and get off this land.

John The Baptist

Lord, I need to be baptized by You.
Why do You come to me?
All my life I looked for You,
and finally You're in front of me.
I'm not worthy to baptize You; I'm a wretched sinner,
but if You would baptize me, I'll become a winner.
So please, my Lord, I beg of You, You baptize me!
Take away my sins, my weaknesses, and set me free.
I will continue to glorify You and praise Your name,
and tell the world of Your love and how You came.
Lord, I only wish to please You and make You proud,
And spread Your name throughout the world,
upon the mountains, and the clouds.

God Is So Powerful

My God, You are so wonderful,
my God, You are so powerful.
Give me but a seed of Your grace,
so that I may keep up with Your pace
To help You win the battle You fought,
for my soul You bravely bought.
It's so easy to sin in this world,
our heads are in a constant swirl.
This world is heartless every day,
but with You there's always a way.
Give me patience, give me faith,
help me win this tiring race.
Give the sign or give the word,
we will move and we will stir.
Be with us to the end of day,
if You do, we'll never stray.
Thank You, God, we praise and sing,
thank You, God, for everything.

Judas

(Remorse)
Why, dear God, does it have to be me?
Why, dear Lord, does the world have to see
that I'm the one that betrayed my Savior?
Why am I the one burdened with that behavior?
Why did You choose me to follow You,
when You knew that I wouldn't be true?
I got to know You so very well,
and now I must, with Your life, sell.
You knew from the beginning that I'm a thief,
Why did You add betrayal to my grief?
My life is hard enough to live that way,
why did You allow me to, with You, stay?
You know with money, I'm so greedy,
you know with the purse I'd take from the needy.
And now we are dealing with a life,
and that life, we know, is Yours, dear Christ.
Please take this burden off my heart,
and maybe a new life I can start.
Why, dear Lord, does it have to be me?
Why, dear Lord, won't You set me free?

Listen To Me

Look at this crowd, what do I do?
I'm so tired looking after you.
You need to listen and listen hard,
for if you do, you will go far.
Repent of your sins and follow what's true,
I can help, but help yourselves, too.
I am the Way, the Truth, and the Light,
I will give you strength to fight the fight.
There will be tribulations and trials for you,
but if you're true to Me, you will get through.
I love you dearly; I'll never be far,
put your foot forward and follow that star.
My Father in heaven will always be there,
He, too, is your Father; He truly cares.
So, listen to Me and listen hard,
follow what I say, and you will go far.

The Lame

Oh, my Lord, how I wish I could walk,
All my life all I could do is talk.
I would sit all day and watch the children play,
And envy them, for I could not even stray.
Why me Lord, why must I be lame?
I'm not asking for much or even fame.
All I ever wanted was to run and climb trees,
All I ever wanted was to be free.
Why me, Lord, what did I do to deserve this?
Look at the fun and the places I missed.
No one else, Lord, can make me walk,
Only you, Lord, can make me walk.

Missing

The body of our Lord has been taken away,
I ran very fast, I could not stay.
I had to tell you what I have seen,
I'm here to take you where I have been.
See for yourself the empty tomb,
feel for yourself all of my gloom.
They've taken Him away! There's no other reason,
for the body of our Lord is now missing.
Why did they do it? Where did they go?
I've searched everywhere, but I don't know.
Come quickly, before they get away!
Come quickly, for we must not delay!
We need to find Him, we need to get Him back,
our faith needs to be strong, it must not lack.
Help us, Father, to see the light,
help us, Father, to fight the fight.

The Blind

As you can see, my Lord, I'm blind,
I'd like to speak to you if you don't mind.
I've been blind since I've been born,
All my life from people I've been scorned.
Of all my sins please forgive me,
And give me the opportunity to see.
Give me the opportunity to see the world,
Let me see the waters swirl.
Thank you, Sir, I can finally see life,
I'm free from worry, I'm free from strife.
Now tell me, Sir, who's this Son of man,
So that I too can worship Him?
Ah yes, Lord, I believe in You,
And now I too can see what's true.

No Turning Back

O my Lord, they're taking You away,
I don't want that; I want You to stay.
I love You dearly, with all my heart,
You're the one who gave me my start.
I pray that I can keep You day by day,
for if I can't, I'll surely stray.
They took away prayer from everyone,
now they want to control religion, I'm stunned.
They worry about one person
who cares not for the old,
from where else can they hear the story be told?
I don't know, Lord, what this world is coming to,
cause at this time we need you each day through.
I don't care what this world says or lacks,
I'm following Jesus, and there's no turning back.

Peter's Pledge

Lord, where are You going? I wish to follow You.
I truly love You, You know that's true.
I'll never leave You to face things alone,
I'll always stand by You as hard as stone.
No matter what happens, I'll always be there,
through thick and thin, I solemnly swear.
So don't worry, my Lord, I'll never stray,
I'm with You, my Lord, all the way.

Peter's Denial

(Despondency)
I followed Him from a distance, even though it was far,
through the gate and courtyard, it was very hard.
I kept going, even though I was cold and tired,
up to the fire I went to get warmed for a while.
What's going to happen on this cold and dreary night?
Will we see Him again in the morning light?
I prayed to God that this would quickly end,
and we would all be back together again.
Then my heart sank as the slave girl asked me,
weren't you with Him, aren't you one of them I see?
No, not I, I said without thinking of the words,
and again, from another, the same question I heard.
You aren't one of His disciples, are you?
Do I have to hear that from you, too?
No, I'm not! Oh no, what did I say once again?
Why is all this falling on me like rain?
Oh what can I do, where can I hide?
Why are they all looking at me?
I'm not the only one that followed Him, can't you see?
Then it comes, the same question,
why do I need to hear it again?
Why can't they leave me alone
and let me ease my pain?
(No) Again I hear the same answer
that came out before,
how badly I wanted to run through the door.
All at once a sound that I never wanted to hear,
and the look from my Lord just filled me with fear.

I have failed Him at a time he needed me the most,
all I wanted was to give up the ghost.
Please, forgive me, Lord, for being so weak,
and help me to find You, for it is You whom I seek.
I know at this time it is hard for You to see
that I truly love You, You're the one for me.
Take me, let me follow You, and take away this strife,
allow me to see You, You are my light.
I love You Lord, yes, truly I do!
Don't let me continue to be such a fool.

Pilate

Pilate was asked to meet with Christ,
Pilate knew he could not be biased.
The governor asked Jesus, "Are You the king of the Jews?
What am I going to do, how can I get rid of You?
Why am I the one to decide on this?
Why can't someone else make this trip?
Don't You hear what they are saying about You?
What can I say, what can I do?"
Then to the crowd, "Which one to release to you,
Barabbas, or Jesus Christ, which will do?"
From his wife, "Don't have anything to do with that man!
in a dream I have suffered a great deal of which I can't
stand."
Back to the crowd, he asked the question as before,
he was tired of the hassle and wanted no more.
"Which of the two do I release to you?"
A decision has to be made, oh what to do.
"What shall I do with Jesus the Christ?"
What must this man pay for a price?"
"Crucify him!" the crowd yelled back,
"Crucify him!" The yelling did not lack.
"What should I do to end this crud?"
Just you know I'm innocent of His blood."

Running Away

(Frailty)
Lord, forgive me for running away,
forgive me for not wanting to stay.
Can't You see I was afraid for my life?
I knew I couldn't handle the strife.
I know You warned us of the coming events,
but we didn't realize or comprehend.
Maybe we should have prepared a while longer,
Then maybe we would've been much stronger.
To see You hanging on the cross at that time
just completely destroyed me and blew my mind.
To see how they treated and punished You,
I wish I had the strength to be there, too.
Lord, forgive me for my plight
and give me the strength for the rest of my life.
To praise Your name and spread it around
throughout the city, countryside, and town.
I truly love You, Lord, don't forget,
for with Your help, there's still hope yet.

What Do We Do

What do we do now, since our Lord is gone?
They have taken Him away, we're all alone.
They've whipped our Lord, and they've crucified Him,
now this battle we fight we'll never win.
What do we do, where do we go?
Without our Lord, we really don't know.
We left everything and everyone to follow our Lord,
and now that He's gone, the fear we have soared.
Most Holy Father, what do we do?
Who do we see, where do we go?
Heavenly Father, why did this have to be?
What are Your plans? Will You help us to see?
Please God, I pray to You,
open our eyes, show us what's true.

The Beatitudes

(Joy)

Happy are those who struggle in the faith,
for the gifts of heaven is their fate.
Happy are those who are humble,
for they will no longer stumble.
Happy are those who are mild, like babes at birth,
for they will become heirs of this earth.
Happy are they who crave to do right,
for they'll be fully rewarded beyond our sight.
Happy are those who show compassion,
for they themselves will receive satisfaction.
Happy is the innocent, free from Satan,
for them, God will be waiting.
Happy are those who for peace we depend on,
for they soon will be known as God's sons.
Happy are those who are oppressed for Godliness,
for in heaven, they'll receive their rest.
Happy are you when people ridicule you,
for as the prophets before you, heaven is yours, too.
These are the beatitudes that we learn,
and great is the reward we receive in return.

We're Here Tonight

(Evensong)
Lord, we're here tonight to learn Your will,
Open our eyes, and our hearts be still.
Help us to understand and be aware
of Your presence and love everywhere.
We need You, Father, more each day,
we need You, Father, in every way.
At times, it's hard to focus on You,
Satan works hard to take us from You.
Help us, Father, to know what's right,
stay with us, Father, through the night.
Teach us where You want us to go,
help us to tell others what we know.
Show us how to tell of Your mercy and love
and the many things that come from above.
There is so much that is pulling us away,
we try so hard not to stray.
So stay with us, Father, and help us fight,
help us to show what is wrong from right.
Help us to understand Your word tonight,
help us to see your glorious light.
Thank You, Father, for Your peace from above,
thank You, Father, for Your patience and love.

You Won't Be Here

(Solicitude)
What do You mean, You won't be here?
what is it that we all will fear?
We don't understand what You're trying to say,
we can't see that, night or day.
Tell us, dear Lord, what You want us to know,
tell us, dear Lord, before You go.
We are afraid to be left alone!
We're afraid of the turmoil that has grown.
Can we help You in any way?
How can we help You to stay?
We're afraid of what we don't know,
we're afraid of what we've been told.
Help us, Jesus, to understand,
tell us where, and how, and when.
If we know and can understand,
we will fight to the very last man.
So what is it that we have to look for?
Is it from the rich or from the poor?
So tell us, Lord Jesus, tell us now,
explain to us all, tell us how.

Acknowledgements

Any published author is surrounded by a team of wonderful people supporting his or her efforts at every turn. I am always thankful to our Lord and Savior, Jesus Christ, for the words that flowed from my pen and landed on your hearts. I also owe a forever debt of gratitude to my chief editor Ashley Hagan and my wife and co-editor Annie "Skip" Harris for content, movement, and structure, and Bayley Holt for the inspirational cover and page design. Not only have these amazing women provided professional guidance, but also encouragement, direction, and support in navigating unfamiliar waters.

I also offer a special note of thanks to my Dad, George F. Harris Sr., for his creative collaboration on the poem sub-titles in the Through Their Eyes section of this book. It is with his great friendship and encouragement that this book was written. I know he is smiling in heaven.

THE

CHATTANOOGA CHOO-CHOO

IT WAS ON MARCH 5, 1880, THAT THE FIRST
PASSENGER TRAIN LEAVING CINCINNATI FOR
CHATTANOOGA WAS NICKNAMED THE
"CHATTANOOGA CHOO-CHOO".
THIS HISTORICAL OCCASION OPENED THE
FIRST MAJOR LINK IN PUBLIC TRANSPORTA-
TION FROM THE NORTH TO THE SOUTH.
THE "CHOO-CHOO" WAS OPERATED BY THE
CINCINNATI SOUTHERN RAILROAD, AMERICA'S
FIRST MUNICIPAL RAILWAY SYSTEM.

Appendix

A. Chapter Pages

- **Family** – The Harris Family from left to right: George Harris Sr., Rose Harris, Jim Harris, George Harris Jr., Lidwina Harris (George Sr.'s mother). (Page 10)
- **Dad** – Coast Guard Commander Jack Dempsey (former world heavyweight champion) talks with First Class Guardsman, George Harris (Sr.) somewhere in the Southeast Pacific during WWII. George Sr. served as a Yeoman on the Coast Guard frigate, the USS Hutchinson, and wrote the ship's newsletter and daily activity schedule. (Page 26)
- **Wife/Partner** – Carole "Skip" "Annie" Harris, George Harris – picture taken at Chickasaw Gardens, Memphis, Tennessee. (Page 34)
- **Friends** – Bill Thompson, Debra Thompson, George Harris taken in their early twenties. These three were, and still are, best friends for around 50 years. George and the Thompsons became friends through Bills older brother who attended high school with George. There is no mistaking the bond shared by these three. (Page 42)
- **Mission Trips** – Love note left by residents of Joplin, Missouri-2012 to those who came to help them rebuild their community. (Page 50)
- **Comfort** – Peaceful sunset picture taken somewhere along the way in George's journey of life. (Page 58)
- **Heroes** – Captain Sheldon Lewis, Woolwich Township Police Department, photo taken at the funeral service of a fallen officer in Delaware. Spending his career in law enforcement, Captain Lewis was responsible for doing many things during his 29 years in law enforcement. Captain Sheldon Lewis finally retired from the Woolwich Township Police Department. Captain was responsible for developing a summer-style boot camp for students at the Kingsway Regional Middle and High

School, and the Gloucester County Prosecutors Office. He also was a physical fitness and Military Drill instructor at the Gloucester County Police Academy known as Rowen University. Captain Lewis's focus was developing social skills and discipline, as he was the first established School Recourse Officer (S.R.O.) in Woolwich Township. He presently teaches the Law Enforcement and Public Safety Program at the Salem County Vocational Technical High School. During George's tenure teaching Radio & TV Broadcasting at Kingsway High School, George and Sheldon, then S.R.O. of the High School/Jr. High, developed an after-school program called Kids Keeping It Real Productions (KKRP) where Sheldon wrote the scripts, and George edited and produced several social awareness movies. As in other programs George taught, the students were the stars who were the actors, camera crew, and additional support in making the movies come alive. George and Sheldon remain the best of friends to this day. (Page 64)

- **Personal Feelings** – George Harris Jr. deep in thought; picture taken by Carole Harris on the beach in Marineland, Florida. (Page 72)
- **Praising God** – The hills of West Virginia, picture taken by George Jr. during a mission trip to that area. (Page 86)
- God Speaking – God's heart that is evident through every storm and every challenge, picture taken by Carole Harris during a daily walk. (Page 104)
- **Biblical Characters** – These characters are just a few that have shown the power and mercy of God. They have left an impression on many a person from generation through generations. (Page 114)
- **Psalms** – Picture of Psalms, New Living Translation Bible, taken by Carole Harris specifically for this publication. (Page 120)
- **Christmas** – The wonder of Christmas is nowhere purer and more evident than in the heart and eyes of a young child; picture of Matthew Harris White, George Jr. and Carole's

grandnephew taken by niece, Brandie Harris. (Page 128)
- **Through Their Eyes** – Cover page of the Through Their Eyes Musical choral parts and music book; lyrics written by George Harris Jr., music written by Carole Harris and Buddy Skipper. You can get a sample of the music on their web page windfallsproductions.com and Facebook page "windfallsproductions". Also you can hear some of their music on YouTube under the same name. (Page 136)

B. **Additional Chapter Pictures**
Family
1. Santa, Jim Harris in Santa's lap, George Harris Jr. standing. (Page 12)
2. Dad playing golf with George Jr. at Penney Retirement Community. (Page 13)
3. Mom, Dad and Jim at Penney Farms Retirement Community. (Page 16)
4. Mom and Dad in front of the St. Augustine, FL home. (Page 17)
5. Mom at the beach in Ocean City, NJ. (Page 20)
6. Dad at the jail used in Tom Sawyer in Hannibal, MO. (Page 21)
7. George Jr. at Penney Retirement Community bench dedicated to Mom and Dad. (Page 22)
8. Jim, Dad, and George Jr. pic taken the day of Mom's celebration of life service. (Page 23)

Dad
1. Mom and Dad on their wedding day in 1943. Soon after, George Sr. shipped out on the USS Hutchinson and the South Pacific during WWII. (Page 33)

Wife/Partner
1. George and wife, Carole Skipper Harris, or known to George as "Annie" taken around 2016. (Page 38)
2. George, "Annie", and Bella the Labrador Retriever taken in their back yard in 2022. (Page 41)

Friends

1. George sharing a laugh with close friend Wild Bill Ingram. Bill joined our household, and our family, in 2012 after completing his degree at Berklee College of Music in Boston. An absolute master at his special brand of outlaw country and his ability to make his wild electric guitar solos wow any audience, he has earned his place as a well-known entertainer /honky-tonk house band in the country music scene on Broadway in Nashville. George and Wild Bill share a special friendship. (Page 46)
2. George and Bill Thompson all dressed up for a fancy affair. (Page 48)
3. George and brother-in-law, Buddy Skipper, during a trip to the Elvis Presley mansion in Memphis, Tennessee. The wall in front of the mansion is notable for its many sentiments of love and devotion to the King of Rock & Roll. (Page 49)
4. Bill Thompson helping George celebrate his 50th birthday at a party in his honor. (Page 49)

Mission Trips

1. George on the ladder during a home repair in Fort Myers, FL. (Page 52)
2. Joplin MO after the 2011 tornado devastation. (Page 53)
3. Joe Barber, George, and another team member on the mission trip to rebuild homes after the tornado in Joplin, MO. (Page 54)
4. Team Member, Ron, cutting wood to repair a storm damaged home in Fort Myers, FL. (Page 55)
5. Team member, Joe Barber, performing partial demolition on a storm damaged home in Fort Myers, FL. (Page 56)

Heroes

1. EMT Carole Skipper Harris (George's wife) assisting a paramedic during a training exercise demonstrating stokes basket rescue maneuvers at Chickies Rock County Park in Lancaster County, PA. The 390-foot decent at this area is often full of vegetation making stokes basket lowering a

challenge while keeping a patient stable. During Carole's six-year service as a radar air traffic controller in the US Navy, she became very interested in search and rescue (SAR) after flying many training and familiarization runs in the CH46 helicopters with the base SAR team. This desire to serve coupled with her strong interest in SAR was proven in the creation of Delaware Valley Search and Rescue (DVRSAR) where she served as President of the BOD. Her dedication was also evident in her seven-year service to Media Fire Company. Created in partnership with Chief Lee Wray and several dedicated members, DVRSAR's five years of existence provided effective search management leadership, navigational support for the K-9 teams (we were the first in our area to offer this service), and ground search tactics. By building our Tri-State Alliance partnership teams that trained together, and training police departments on how effective our teams could be, we were called out by local police, State police, and the FBI on over 400 searches in our five- year existence. (Page 66)

2. Guardsman George Harris Sr., picture taken in "boot camp" soon before he would take his lovely Rose's hand in marriage, and take the trip of his lifetime on board the U.S.S. Hutchinson as the frigate set sail as part of the Pacific fleet during WWII. (Page 68)

3. Carole Skipper Harris practicing her rappelling techniques. As a team Member with DVRSAR, we trained monthly on all aspects of search and rescue including map & compass, K-9 navigational support, high angle rescue (rappelling, injured/non-injured person rescue, rope haul systems used to lower gear/raise people), search management skills, and ground search techniques in various terrain. (Page 70)

4. A younger pic of Sheldon as Sargent Sheldon Lewis, USMC. His unit provided logistics for Transportation Management responsibilities. His time in service included

both the Beirut and Granada conflicts. (Page 71)

C. **The End**

Picture taken in front of the Chattanooga Choo Choo located in Chatanooga, TN. (Page 160)

D. **Back Cover**

Picture of George Harris Jr. taken in his younger years.